Henrik Nordbrandt

ARMENIA

translation:
Henrik Nordbrandt & Alexander Taylor

curbstone press

cover photo:
Bjarne Stig Hansen

this publication has received support
from the following:
THE DANISH MINISTRY OF CULTURE
THE AUGUSTINUS FOUNDATION
CONNECTICUT COMMISSION ON THE ARTS
 a state agency whose funds
 are recommended by the
 governor and appropriated by
 the state legislature

ARMENIA was originally published in 1982
by Gyldendal Forlag, Copenhagen, Denmark

LC: 84-7787
ISBN: 0-915306-41-7
Danish ISBN: 87-7456-957-0

distributed in
Denmark by:
VINDROSE FORLAG
14 Nybrogade
DK 1203 Copenhagen K
Denmark

CURBSTONE PRESS 321 Jackson Street Willimantic, CT 06226

CONTENTS

I

II

I

It urur, kervan yurur
The dog barks, the caravan wanders

I sit on a wall gazing out over walls and walls
while I have the feeling that my shadow
is on the way across the polished stones of empty squares
    or halfway up
the yellow-plastered church facades hang head downwards
    when the bells begin noisily tolling.

At night everything seems to move on winding stairs:
Even the saints' images hanging in the doorway arches
    between burning lamps
descend slowly in increasingly smaller circles
under the stars which become distinct as if seen from the bottom
    of a deep well on a plateau.

And here I know that a random glance will use me
    as its periscope
and when dawn's shadows hastily creep forward
across tents and cold fireplaces, discover a black bird
which takes off from a pole, emits a complaining cry
    and flies east toward Yerevan.

Rows of wax candles: Armenia has gone its way
    with its names and its stones.
Now a child whispers the names, now a platoon of soldiers
    take turns moving the stones
and the hand you reach into the dark of the room
comes burnt into sight outside in the sunlight of the courtyard
where you sit on a dead horse writing:
    You write it in the sand
with a shaking finger, and in the snow with a bone
and you write it on the last dazzling wall
    before spring
when the wall is about to collapse, and your fever
rises like the quickly rising roll of drums:
The second and the third division are now already
    burying the first
        you are on your way into the fourth
and the fourth already lays bare the teeth of the fifth.
Rows of soldiers become rows of sunbeams
    in which the dust dances
and the letter with the three seals changes invisible hands
    the gilt-edged letter
where it is written that the letter shall go farther.
The children who were born the day you departed
now sit on cold clay floors and learn it by heart.
Their chanting reaches you across the Turkish-blue waters of the lakes
    while from rows of mountains
rows of binoculars are aimed at rows of binoculars
and rows of empty holes stare at rows
    of empty holes.
The priests count them and strike them from the text.
The consonants fall out of the names, the drums roll.
Stones change hands with letters and letters with stones.
    Along the road to Ararat
the flies sweat a filthy layer across the earth.

As the day gradually darkens, you fix your glance more steadily
on the demolished walls of houses by the river bed
and the closed books, which you read by the sunflicker
while your nervous hand never manages to rest
long enough to confirm the fleeting outline of things.

The wind rises. And the light disappears from window after window
with your advancing shape, which dooms
the streets to an increasingly more unrecognizable return
when the names which are called out in the dark square
have no faces to confirm them, and moments.

O you, who in heaps of old eyeglasses are the last
glance back across the brown fields, striped by snow
in heaps of clothes the bitter cold early in March
and on doors the pale marks after removed nameplates
the hour you yourself can only knock on a child's sleep.

Don't force me to walk, restless, over the bridges any more
searching after a sure sign from you, still a
ruined object: Give me your tattered feather costume to die in
and crush me against the day's outermost wall, where the roses
are shaken violently by strong gusts of wind from the northeast . . .

To look out across the snow and drum the table restlessly
is to trade eyes with death and feel them roll
        and trading eyes with death
is to use your skull like a crucible
        and think lead
while you vomit your insides tangled in barbed wire
without being able to free yourself from your century-old nausea:
        Thousand of lead bullets
for each eyesocket which has wished to copulate
        with a green star
and just as many soldiers on each cracked windowpane
which rattling stares out into the night frost
when the facades can only show how somebody has gone wrong
        or sunk into the earth:
Through the holes they have left you look into a forest
        where a low winter sun
falls rose-pink over the snowbound paths and glades
and you stagger to meet your snowbound heart through a misfocused
        pair of binoculars
while a circle of generals have already taken aim:
Ten thousand shots for each heart which has trembled
        in union with the foliage
before the snow begins to melt from lips and eyelashes
        and the forest to walk:
The forest walks faster than a child can count the trees
and roots clasp the bones in your hand before you have written
        half of your name:
Hundreds of thousands of names go into each forest before the snow
        covers the tracks
and the houses are left standing with their shiny facades
                and cold chimneys
while the windows rattle like answers to a letter never mailed
        whose lines erase you
as if you had never been here to write it . . .

And you stare out over the snow trading eyes with death
and see the uniform drop from your skeleton when you turn your back
to the table in the glade
where obsolete maps, held down by shell fragments and stones
flap sadly in the evening wind.

It happens now and then, when I stand here not knowing
        what I'm waiting for
that someone has been here again and again trying in vain
        to transform these lines
into a piano sonata, whose absence the river's lazy waters
        make even more distinct
so that packs of wild pigs have to fill the forest with their screams
while I lean against the bridge railing
in order to contemplate whether I can stand reality:
        So that's what it's like
having only your own philosophy to go by
and having to alter it incessantly, so changeable
        the weather is here
and so far from Mount Ararat's snow clad peak
it suddenly strikes me. And like Chopin
        it was naturally it
I thought I should finally get to see
        when we arranged this
but then it was only you who was standing in the open kitchen door
smiling enigmatically, as you've always done
all these years it has taken me to come by
        with cigarettes and beer
and suggested that I start over, completely over
even though you knew very well that's what I do
        all the time.

And just as I write this without even having been here
        someone has probably
become hopelessly involved in this dream again
now that I myself am awakened and more distinct than ever
        painfully distinct
out here midway on the bridge between the slaughterhouse and forest
        observed by my witnesses
by the vulture which sailed slowly down the river
        on a bloated stomach of a cow
the soldiers on a dusty drilling ground behind the mosque
and the girl who ran into the forest after a ball
        and never came back
—my wife, my psychiatrist, my daughter's teacher—
while the same hand that began to play
can now only strike the same key
        over and over
and the dream of Ararat plagues me, like the music of Chopin
and the bridge is without end and without beginning.

II

I want to get out, but of what I don't know.
Of stone or water: Neither of the two
can fathom the depth of the other
but where they are confused, a huge prison takes shape
where every logical thought burns itself up
        in scream and mirror:
Mirror turned toward mirror: Mirror for Justinian
and for Theodora with the wide mouth.
Two rulers have turned their eyes toward the East:
        A mosaic laid in a wall in the West
in which eleven cities have been besieged and plundered
and burned to glaze, while a twelfth still stands:
Jerusalem of stone and water doubly confused
        giant mirror toward the light
ship only seeming to move
because everyone is always disembarking
and the desert wind snaps against the stones like a sail
        of silk:
Stone by stone, and the sound of the water
from the other side of the stones, heard through them:
        Mirror
for the spring, wherein blossoming fruit trees
blend with the pomp of the fighting rulers.
And I, the confined one, warm my hands
over a fire that burns on the snow from last year
        while with a bone I
draw pictures of windows and doors in the snow.
        Three walls
I have built for you by listening to the water:
One so you can find yourself with your shadow
and one to show you the way: The third you only discover
        when you arrive.
Since to be precise is no longer my concern
        but to be intense.

And if I lead you astray, it's because you yourself
from the beginning have asked to be led astray:
A.J.E.X.Q.H. Incomprehensible inscriptions on walls
and uninscribed remains of walls along the road: These
        are the holes in the structure
(The seventeen kingdoms which have annihilated each other)
with the help of which we recognize the ground
        on which we still stand
and plant trees as if we still believed in a future
and listen to the words we whisper to each other
        in the darkness
A. for Alexander, J. for Jenghis, E. for Enver
        and X.Q.H. for the borders
which change places continually like the languages
which overlap each other and are confused.
Choose any letter you like, hurry and choose
        before it disappears
and I will show you the color that the earth takes on
when your blood sinks among the spring flowers
        and the stones.
Stone upon stone: We, too, somebody whispers
        from inside the stones, are prisoners of history,
our flesh the mortar of history. A fast river
which the stream of blood has made faster
        flows toward the East
when by means of the blossoming trees under the snows of Ararat
the rotten timbers and the grass on the roof
        I recognize the house
where we sleep on floors of stone, to the sound of water
after the daily toil of planting trees
        and digging graves.

As often as I do not return
　　　it is Armenia
I do not return to
—as the journey I never begin
makes more tired and a little disheartened
when I myself am lying asleep
—as those chains wear which I only feel
when at dawn I am awakened by the melancholy
　　　traveling inside me
like a broken spearhead, dipped in poison,
—and it is Armenia who bangs her head
　　　against that wall
where I wasn't able to leave
the sign which could have saved her, who is now
tortured instead of me in her soiled prison
and prevented the son who is born as often
　　　as I do not return
from tearing his mother's throat.
　　　O my place!
The place where I long to be used
by this confused I, which would cast off
all its disguises if it could
the place where I age like a trousseau
which lies rotting in a drawer
and where a stone with my name on it already lies.
　　　I want to get out!
Show me who I am in return for these
　　　fragmentary messages
smuggled past the censor, camouflaged as poems
which Enver's henchmen cannot decipher.
Bring these bones to silence, which so long
　　　have howled like a watchdog
by the gate of a strange man's property
—or drown them with the sound of your rivers!

The East seen as a mirror for the West:
Rows of sails, rows of prows of ships
and old Homer's mumbling as background
Germanic drums and Pound's blind rage
(Blind as a bat, blind as a bat).
        Again and again
we Greeks, Romans, Goths and Slavs
are those who stumble over one another, where mirror
        meets mirror.
Soon there'll be no more room
the space become too narrow and too hot
and there will be no way out: One kingdom falls
and the next takes over its blind corridors
and invisible breach: There is no space
        between the mirrors.
I want to get out: Alexander and Justinian
mirror for Alp Arslan and Timur Lenk
Timur Lenk mirror for Enver Pasha
mirror for Hitler: We are all followed
        by mirrors
with which we send signals to each other
through the centuries, the milleniums
over the continents: But what good does it do
to have once looked into a mirror
which has perceived the image of a mirror
in which Confucius beheld himself! From Berlin
        to Peking
heaps of skulls lie about
left by those who learned nothing.

And in the middle of it all
in the middle of stretches of continents and time:
    The fruit orchard Armenia
where conversations could take place under the trees
    even when circumstances were worst
and images are cut into solid walls
    for the delight of the eye.

Blind as a bat
am I, too:
But who has seen a bat
fly into anything!
We secretaries and eunuchs
who flutter about here
at the Sultan's court
and sleep with our heads downward
hanging over a pit
of boiling tar
hear by means of the whispering
which emerges from secret corridors
where spies
spy on spies
by means of slander
and slanders of slander
—so keenly, that we always know
precisely where we are
and what sudden dangers
are approaching us.

And in the same way
this overburdened language
this mixture of Turkish
Arabic and Persian
which gradually the poets
are barely able to use
—in the act of eradicating itself
as it in fact is—
tells us beneath all its complicated expressions
quite simply about how quickly
the colossus on clay feet is falling.

Your name, Enver Pasha
is a corruption
of the Arabic word "anwar"
superlative of "munir"
"The Lightgiving."
But never has anything darkened the world
as totally as your light
and never have I seen history
as extinct
as when you walked through it.

May your name maintain its superlative
in Hell, too.
May you stay in the flames
"The Most Lightgiving."

Enver Pasha seen as a mirror for me
is not an image I have thought out
or enjoy thinking of
        but something
which was whispered to me in a dream
just as I was about to wake up.
But now the words are out of my mouth
my eyes immediately demand to participate
while my head with an involuntary movement
forces them away from the inevitable
and out toward the light over the Golden Horn:
        I want to get out
I say again and beat my fist on the window sill.
But no quite so discursive fantasy
is ready to carry me away
from this lurid place, where braziers
are glowing, surrounded by shivering watchmen
        in the growing darkness
which continuously lessens the distance
between the terrible mirror and me:
        And thus
it suddenly occurs to me
that in fact Enver must often have stood
fantasizing about Alexander and Ceasar
Alp Arslan and Jenghis
as a refuge from the images of dead Armenians
the hosts of dead Armenians
who must have filled the darkness around him
with their groaning and dissolved contours.

Verily! Enver, too, is my mirror!
—I, who have used so many mirrors
with so much crafty ingenuity
in order to avoid seeing the place which holds
      my senses together
while I warmed myself a little by these images
      in Byzantine colors
— I too share the responsibility for all those
      now being annihilated
in the dark, to which fearful I turn my back
      the black hellflames
from Armenia, Germany, Uganda and Cambodia . . .
      all those places
of which we learn nothing until history places them
      and us each in its scale.

The place that holds my senses together
        in my consciousness:
If I saw it my limbs would be torn apart
and fly off in all directions.
But whether I want to avoid seeing it
or whether I want to see it
        I don't know
and soon this knowledge is my only luggage
on these planless journeys in the East and West
where I have learnt in several languages
        that language
is nothing but a sieve with coarse holes
in the hands of a thirsting soul
        one which tries to collect
in the desert a mouthful of drinking water
        from the dew:
The morning star tells me how precisely
        I have failed again
but never what it was that left
a cryptic, hastily written message
on a piece of paper in one of my pockets
or cut a deep scratch on my cheek
without my noticing it when it happened.
        O my place!
Where nomadic tribes become residents
and residents are driven out into deserts
        to die of thirst
just when their nomadic souls have become accustomed
        to walls of stone.
—I have built a house for you, O my place
        a fragile house of wood
so that you shall feel neither confined
        nor entirely unprotected.

But as often as I turn my back
you set fire to the house to warm yourself
just as I thoughtlessly warm myself
        in these images
—images of rulers on their way from the West to the East
in order to forget what huge powers
also make me homeless and unconscious
where those who once lived in the house now
appear as black holes in each other's consciousness.
—And meanwhile the German Kaiser
in cooperation with the pashas, Enver, Talaat and Jemal
        plans the murder of the Armenians.

Roots, what have I to do with roots!
I want to send my own roots down
from the treetops on which I float
        and I can!
My forefathers—and mothers were Chinese,
Jews, Assyrians, Malays, and Bantus.
I sat at one of the oars
when the ships sailed against Troy
listened to Confucius
and fought with Fatih Sultan Mehmet
when he took Constantinople.

I was the first to write
        every poem, too:
It was the others who imitated me.

If one day you should go into San Vitale
        you will hear me
standing at your side, explaining what you see.
        Because I was the one
who made the picture of Justinian and Theodora
and while I think of it, I was also the one who
whispered to old Julius
what to say when he crossed the Rubicon.

If it suits me, and it does,
        I will declare
Armenia my homeland
and at the same moment always have been there.
And if someone should call all this postulating
I can only laugh at them, poor fools
who talk about roots but can't even
tell the difference between earth and fertilizer.

By the flames from the burning Armenia
I thaw out my frozen hands
    and seize my pen:
As many wings as I myself
have burnt up in my longing for Van and Yerevan
it seems to me this fire is my right.
And you, Armenia, I've given
these paper houses for your glance to recognize
which always seems unable to find rest:
It's better for you to live this way
without furniture, superfluous as it is anyway
when the soldiers come and break down your door
and better for you to sleep between two sheets of paper:
The light sleep you get then is your best weapon
—but not to sleep at all probably serves you best:
To move sleepless, your senses sharpened
    to their breaking point
and to live on the berries and the roots you can find
in your dark and damp hiding places:
That way you will be able to survive a little longer
    until help reaches you.
You don't answer! Perhaps you think I'm mocking you
—as you have been mocked and abused
    so many times already
and have to kneel down crying at each cross-road
    stigmatized and bleeding.
But read further: There's no help on the way.
The world has turned a deaf ear to your screams
and even history considers forgetting you.
Before long you will never have been
and no one will ever have heard your name
or mirrored his soul in your images
made with such great love: Your only way out
    is wily cunning.

That's why I tease you and deceive you
so as to teach you the art of deception
—the art of lying in ambush and cutting the enemy down
    from behind.
You have used up too much strength building walls
planted too many trees behind the walls
and gotten yourself inebriated on too much flowerscent
    from well laid out gardens
and on too much poetry for what these things are worth:
Now it's time you begin to live like the nomad
    that you too once were
while your enemy sinks down his roots and falls asleep
in Habez' rose-garden, where the nightingale sings
    and the waterpipe bubbles.

When a people are driven into exile
and spread across the continents,
in the course of a few generations there is
less and less difference
between the eyes of their sons and daughters
—as if their ability to observe
the same place in the universe
grew larger and larger
with the increased distance
and with the time which passed
since their forefathers and mothers
turned their backs to it.

Why, I don't know
but it also
fits the linguistic theory
which claims that the language
that's spoken farthest from its source
is nearest to the source.

I've often observed this
in the old capitals of Europe
as well as in New York
—but seen it clearest
in Jerusalem's glowing evening light
and in the violet gleam
which envelops Ararat in spring.

A.J.E.X.Q.H.: The sudden connections
which arise when I sit writing
make me dizzy and melancholy at the same time:
So many hands have laid stone upon stone
    into this wall
which divides me from the gleaming waters
    on their way toward Gibraltar
that my own hand feels powerless
and keeps lying on the table like a dead thing
    a stone.
But as all water in its shifting shapes
is one and eternally bound through the cracks of the stones
    and the air
so language is, too: And I've scarcely thought this
before an Arabic proverb occurs to me
like an ironic commentary on my words:
    "A wall
is better than a thousand good connections."
Truly, the nomad's dream of walls was our
    mistake, too.
We have stared ourselves blind on these surfaces of stone
    so richly ornamented
and sung ourselves deaf in Hafez and Khayyam.
Mehmet knew this, and before Mehmet, Jenghis
    Alp Arslan and Alexander:
Gleaming harnesses, ships' prows shaped like dragons
it is I now see when I squint
into the glaring sunlight above the Golden Horn
    crossed by so many conquerors:
We should have invested in horses and ships
    instead of walls
in connections instead of a peaceful life.
Soon we won't be able to use the walls for much else
    than writing on:

E. for Enver, X. Q. H. for the borders, which aren't strengthened
     but eradicated by walls:
They are nothing but houses of paper, which burning
can only illuminate individual, detached images
     of history:
The soldiers, who now are trained by German officers
     down there in the courtyard
or long lines of refugees, observed
by some random European traveler
     from a compartment window
in a train he doesn't know contains confidential
papers to the Kaiser in Berlin . . .
papers whose contents have already been converted
into bloody actions far within Armenia
where a bird, bewildered and screaming, circles
     over a sea of manes.

When nomads settle down
inner walls are transformed into outer
and fear into melancholy
their songs lose their narrative
and become sad
with afterthought, which can do nothing
other than walk in and out of doors
and they begin to die
a new death, the personal
petty death, which I fear and hate
the one which is like a pawnbroker:
And demands everything, even your clothes.

Nothing can make me so sad
as a well-kept garden.
Each one gives off a layer
of sneaking growths, greedy fingers
over my soul
drowns it in terrible greenhouses
and steals my heart without killing me
but keeps me half-doped
like the spider its living prey.
The flourishing farms I have seen
spread out over certain deserts
remind me of terrible, green bulletholes.

Armenia is the place we've all been
        and then forgotten about it:
The place we glimpse on our way
        into sleep
and in a different light when we leave it:
These moments, which are so fragile
we can't wrest the least thing from them
        without destroying them utterly.
Yes, to see Armenia as a soap-bubble
        or eggshell
is probably the safest, if you want to go on
the best way to sneak up on her:
Now you are already so much farther
that you can turn your back to the soap bubble
think of something else and listen to the owls:
You can distinguish the screech of three owls
through the soft darkness of the spring evening:
Two of them are mating, the third is sitting now
on the Emperor's shoulder, whispering to him
what it has experienced on its way:
Burning cities and nations in migration
all the way from the Baltic Gulf and out
        to the borders of China:
Before long Armenia will once more be assaulted
        and raped:
In what other way did you think that someone like you
        would be brought into the world:
Your fathers are Goths, Mongols, Indians
        Turks and Arabs
and also he who sat on the doorstep
up in Scandinavia blowing soap bubbles
while the owls screeched from the forest.
The rape of three continents runs in your veins:

Now you are inside the egg
inside the soap bubble, in a terrible room
where everything is a mirror and continually seems
    to be coming toward you
with furious speed, but without ever striking.
    I want out, you scream
and the soap bubble breaks, the egg cracks.
But to be inside and outside at the same time
is really what you want
to dream, sunk in an unborn substance
while you observe everything from outside
analyzing soberly: No one can do that.
Now you are back on the cold doorstep
    with the soapwater
listening to the owlscreech from the forest and dreaming
as you have done for 50 years, about the priest's
    16-year-old daughter.
In your attempt to sneak up on Armenia
    you've been snuck up on yourself
and you, who had your whole life before you
when you began this, now you are old
and haven't come a step nearer Armenia.
It's the fault of the owls, and the soap bubbles:
They are every bit as seductive as the dreams
one wastes his life on by returning to
    again and again.
I can't see because of you. You block
    the light.
But if you will do me the favor
of moving just a little so I can see
the road that ends out in the mist at the foot of Ararat
I will show you the snow clad peak.
    If nothing else
so you can understand the strange words
you have on your lips now and then when you waken.

Blind me. Put out my eyes
so I can't see history
in any other light than memory's
—that light, which is so poor
that it only has strength enough to shine
on the simplest and most necessary things:

That light, which gets the needle in the haystack
to shout its hiding place
and from the kitchen door ajar
falls out across the dunghill
whose contents tell so much more
than the news and the President's
        last speech.

Out of what: Of sleep or sleeplessness.
So indefinable the borders have become
that it's hardly possible to go
more than once through the same door.
And the woman who stands there with the light behind her
calls me by a new name
every time she needs a mirror.
Breathe on me! I say, tired and irritated
I no longer care to tell you
which dress best becomes you.
Then she breathes defiantly, and I perish in dew
and the memory of bat wings
torn out of sleep: My heart, it is
which is melting the ice of the little lake
where the city orchestra has now taken its place
and begins to blow into its brass
while a large bear dances in the foreground:
To wakem myself in this way is the art
that's taken me the longest to learn
but interpreting the symbols I gladly
        leave to you
whose curiosity is so insatiable.
Out of sleeplessness I've created this door
you can use it as you wish.
I'm tired of carrying it and just wish
        to sleep again
but if I were you, I would probably
hire a maid to go out of it first.
        The times are uncertain
and what I'm writing here, I myself have hardly
        any control over
so many there are whispering to me.

Some ceremony or other is always
involving me against my will
here where you are nothing more than a dumb tourist
who's only traveling to photograph himself
        in front of the sights:
But the priest, now making the sign of the cross
and the clown, too, the snake charmer and the pimp
        are me
and I am he who dances in public squares and markets
bedecked with empty tin cans:
In shifting disguises I trick sleep
        and approach
the place where I long to be used
the place where my dreams can manage
        without me
and where my invisible chains will fall.
Stay with me a while! Sing a song for me!
If I collapse, you'll have to put your own
blindfold on and feel your way forward.
So raw as your fingertips have become
you'll soon find your way to the plateaus
        which I'm longing for
and understand why I've deceived you so long
and let all the doors stand open on whining hinges
        in the spring wind.

When I look at Ararat
I feel God's presence.
I know
he's looking at me
and imagine that he's saying:
To what use
have I created all this cheap trash
all this fucking disorder.

But I also know
that there are spring days
where God descends into a person
looks at the mountain and says:
Praised be man
and glorified on an earth like this
which can simultaneously
be totally purple and totally green.

The dog barks
the caravan moves on
and the eye of the needle
which its camels snuck up on
stares at the stars, forgiving everything.
In the hands of a woman
who fell asleep over her work
I leave my threads.

Water bound by stone, stone bound by water:
        In this way everyone
who has strength to see therein uses
Jerusalem as a mirror for his own imprisonment:
        Mirror for David
and for Titus, too: Mirror for Jews
        and for Arabs
who are no more than each other's hostages
        and just as unfree
as river and riverbed: The dusty Mount Zion
        mirror for Armenia
which is the mirror in which I most often sense
the presence of a place on earth
where a single sunbeam would be able to undo
        all my bonds:
Mirror for death: Images of birds
hewn into the Armenian walls all the way
        from Jerusalem to Yerevan:
Images of dancers: Europe and Asia
linked by chains of dancers
        these
are the hostages: The Armenians the Kurds' hostage
the Kurds the Turks' and the Turks the Germans' . . .
And each hostage killed before his own wall
        and afterwards depicted on the wall
from the beginning of time and to this hour
where the birds fly screaming toward the north
over the walls and all the streaming waters.

It is thus we have built Babel, the Pyramids
        and the confused Europe
which collapses while we continue building
        for the day
when we'll look out over a huge ocean of trash:
        Mirror for God
who is praised now up in the Armenian quarter
with a noise which doesn't give me the peace to think.
Jerusalem! I have begun to believe that you are God's
        prison on earth.

Neither of stone nor water: It is trash
from which history would rather build its monuments
And as often as we lose the overview
the point rises like the round tower
    in the fairy tale:
A kilometer high, inverted well without sides
    stuffed full of trash
a triumphal arch of junk, a fecal pipette:
    Flesh that goes on living
in a new condition, where noisily chomping
and belching it pushes forward toward its place:
The dead which feed the dead with their dead flesh
in the gaps within the displayed trash:
The whole of classic art, and all the mess
as well as the series of discoveries:
The Cannon, the Guillotine and the fallen Skylab
glued together with flesh: History's mortar
which we mix day and night sunk down in a
    yeasting disintegration
of pent-up dreams and distorted reality:
    Triumphal arch for Titus
over the conquered and destroyed Jerusalem
triumphal arch of skulls for Jenghis
and of eyeglasses and dentures for Enver and Hitler:
Mirror turned toward mirror, where only the dark
is allowed to observe itself:

Triumphal arches of darkness
through which we have come through time
gratefully blinded and led astray
all the way from China, through the Middle Ages
Islam and the flowering Armenia
in order to stand before this miserable tower
this dunghill watered by all the rivers of the world
all the power plants and all the pissing murderers:
Death's pipette
which has already started shadowing the sun.

It's getting so that we part more often than we meet
and the roads insist on going north without predecessors
to warn the birds in the evergreen forests
and the frogs in the swamps. At the markets of the great crossroads
we get less and less for the wares we sell
and pay more and more dearly. Each of our movements
seems to carry us farther away
from something which continuously becomes less definable
in proportion to the distance to it
which our defeatist attitude intensifies
—and thereby heavier. That's the explanation for
the youngest of them already imagining it
as a shrine stuffed with treasures
although it's known first and foremost for its emptiness
and they've begun to praise it, too, in new songs
which are poor copies of the old ones. Because in exile
all the patterns bleed in a coarse repetition
mistakes are hidden under a cheap imitation of gold
the chisel slips and the stone breaks into pieces
while the guardians of tradition get fat, take over
the temple of a foreign religion as well as their courtesans
and buy into the slave markets.
In the long drawn-out strophes we once learned
there is still a melancholy reverberation of bells
which keeps hanging in the air over darkening bays
where expensive wares are sailing into the harbor under silk sails
a jetty, a farm, a door and a stairway.

But the rudder is missing, the key has been lost
we can't write our names in our own language
and the cord won't hold. Our music is dying
for lack of care and therein resembles history
that which gradually turns into a feeling of loss
and thus intensifies the danger of an unforeseen repetition
when its details are eradicated: Its most intense expression
is the wild dances you execute dressed in gaily-colored rags
always evasive, disappearing, on your way out into the darkness.

Every time I attempt a new style
    I see you briefly
and lose you again with a new emphasis.
And maybe it is exactly that weakness
    that is my style:
To write these letters to you, Armenia
is like cheating oneself at solitaire:
Every time I win, every time I feel
by the trembling of my hand that I have lost
when I draw these pictures in cold ashes
pictures of windows where the same faces
keep appearing: Alexander
Theodora, Alp Arslan, Jenghis, Enver . . .
    For a glimpse of you
I'd gladly stake all my houses of cards
but the night on the plateau is cold
    so I sell you
to the soldiers for an old blanket
and warm my hands over your burning letters
    so full of accusations.
Believe me, these lines too are nothing
but a new way of misleading you
    a new deceit.
So much for love, so much for poetry.
Those whom I deceive are always those whom I love.
My horses I sell for a prison wall
my connections for a beautiful stone
and my homeland for the smell of its flowers.
Terrible is this earth! But I know how
I shall make you listen
and now you are there again in the doorway
the door banging in the wind
or think that you are there in your bewilderment:

Don't you understand
that you've been sold, raped, killed
and forgotten by the world for time and eternity, too.
The only thing
I can offer you is this cracked mirror
and ask you to put on your most beautiful dress
in the hope that then you will notice the bulletholes.

LIST OF NAMES

Alexander. Alexander the Great (356-323 B.C.).

Alp Arslan, Muhammad 'ibn Da'ud (ca. 1030-1072). The Selchuk dynasty's second sultan. In a battle at Manizkirt in Anatolia in 1070 he defeated the Byzantines under King Romanos IV Diogenes. The battle assured the Turks continued supremacy in Anatolia.

Ararat. Armenia's holy mountain.

David. The Biblical King David.

Enver. Enver Pasha (1881-1922). Turkey's Minister of War from 1914-1918. During these years Turkey was ruled by a triumvirate of Enver, Talaat and Jemal (Cemal).

Hafez, Shemseddin Muhammad (-1389). Iranian poet.

Jenghis. Jenghis Khan (1162-1227). Mongolian conqueror.

Jemal (Cemal). Jemal Pasha (1872-1922). See under Enver.

Julius. Julius Caesar. (100-44 B.C.).

Justinian. (483-565). Byzantine emperor.

Khayyam. Omar Khayyam (1048?-1122), Iranian poet.

Mehmet. Fatih Sultan Mehmet, Mehmet the Conqueror. (Reigned from 1451-1481.) Conquered Constantinople in 1453.

Pasha. In Ottoman history the highest title given to civilian or military officials.

Pound. Ezra Pound (1885-1972). American poet.

S. Vitale. Church in Ravenna (completed 546-548). Famous for its mosaics of the Byzantine Emperor and Emperess, Justinian and Theodora.

Talaat. Talaat Pasha (1874-1921). See under Enver.

Theodora. Byzantine Emperess (-548). Emperor Justinian's wife.

Timur Lenk. Tamerlane (1336-1405). Tartar conqueror.

Titus. Roman Emperor (81-39 B.C.).

Van. The name of a province and a lake in Turkey.

Yerevan. The capital of the Armenian Soviet Republic.